# TRINA TURK

CHRONICLE CHROMA

for jonathan

# foreword

There are certain clichés that persist about Southern California fashion—that it's all surf wear, denim, and Hollywood red-carpet glitz. But during her twenty-five-year career, Trina Turk has managed to transcend them all, harnessing the mood-lifting power of color, natural landscape, modernist art, and architecture to give California a richer sense of its aesthetic self—and make the world want to come here.

Born in San Francisco, Turk spent her early childhood in California before her father, a cosmetics industry executive, moved the family to the Seattle area. But her time here made quite an impression, and all through high school and college she was aching to get back.

Her mother, who is Japanese, taught her to sew at age eleven, and her first project was making a halter top. From then on, Turk knew she wanted to study fashion. After earning a degree in apparel design from the University of Washington, her first job at Brittania Jeans in Seattle involved trips to Asia, initiating a love of travel. She moved back to Los Angeles in 1985 to work for Ocean Pacific, designing colorful prints and color-block board shorts. Her next job was designing a short-lived sportswear collection for swimwear label Anne Cole. When that folded, Turk moved to working for junior sportswear companies.

But she always wanted to work for herself and turn her love of California into something more sophisticated—inspired by resort living, poolside cocktails, and casual, artistic elegance. When she started her own line in Los Angeles in 1995, it consisted of bright-colored silk doupioni separates screen printed with giant photographic prints of flowers. A multi-brand retailer placed a $250K order, financing the company's first year.

Turk was still honing her design vocabulary. She bought some yardage of vintage silk jersey in fun prints and made simple drawstring skirts and button-down shirts. When Fred Segal snapped them up, she realized she had something. Prints became the brand's calling card. Turk designs forty-five to fifty new prints each year at her headquarters in Los Angeles, where much of the production is still done locally.

In the late 1990s, Turk helped put Los Angeles fashion on the map, leading a wave of contemporary designers who were changing the way women shopped and dressed by offering elevated style at a price young people could afford. Unlike so many others, she's weathered the storm of the recession, 9/11, and the changing retail environment by having a sure sense of her brand identity and carefully diversifying into licensed categories.

Over time, Turk's collections have been inspired by everything from a polyester flea market find; and Palm Springs modernist architecture; to art and design heroines Anni Albers, Eileen Gray and Sonia Delaunay, the women of the Bauhaus. Her style icons are strong women like herself: Iris Apfel, Millicent Rogers, Audrey Hepburn, Mary Tyler Moore, Jacqueline Kennedy Onassis, Gloria Steinem, Diana Vreeland, and Peggy Moffitt. All of them were able to mix chic and casual—something Turk strives for in all of her designs, from a floaty printed silk caftan or a pair of cropped cigarette pants to a jacquard boatneck top.

One of the hallmarks of her brand has been its affiliation with Palm Springs—Turk knew it was cool before the Ace Hotel did. In 1998, she and her late husband, Jonathan Skow, bought a house in the desert city that would become the brand's spiritual center. (Turk, the designer, and Skow, the photographer, the two were a golden couple, soaking up every cultural reference and moment but never translating it into their work too overtly.) A 1936 Streamline Moderne style inspired by a sea vessel, their Ship of the Desert second home, became the canvas for a growing lifestyle of kaleidoscope prints and cocktail dreams, including swimwear, menswear, accessories, and home design—as well as for collaborations with Macy's, Banana Republic, Disney, F. Schumacher & Co., an updated Malibu Barbie with Mattel, and more.

In 2002, Turk opened a boutique on Palm Springs' North Palm Canyon Drive, which became a catalyst for the district's stylish renaissance. The building was designed by modernist architect Albert Frey (who also designed city hall), with the original interior decorated by Kelly Wearstler, and an expansion in 2012 fashioned by Bestor Architecture. It has become a destination in itself, selling the designer's own collections next to books, art pieces, and home accessories by Missoni, MQuan Studio, Jonathan Adler, Alexandra von Furstenberg, Joe Cariati, and more.

While many have mined Palm Springs for inspiration, Turk's affection has come with authenticity and support: she's become an ambassador in the media for the best hotels, vintage stores, and restaurants, and an avid modernism conservationist working as a member of the Palm Springs Modern Committee and the Palm Springs Art Museum. She and Skow helped to fund the purchase of the building for the Palm Springs Art Museum Architecture and Design Center, which celebrates the area's design treasures.

Not limited to California, Turk's love of travel and adventure has also taken her to Havana, Capri, Jaipur, Marrakech, and beyond—always on the hunt for a new color palette, paisley, or print. Her power is in the ability to make every day a vacation, her clothing steeped in interesting references but never pretentious. It always makes you feel good, like the first burst of sunshine after you step off the plane in California, for which she will forever be a cheerleader.

**booth moore**

Clockwise from top left: Trina Turk's parents Michie Sugimoto and Jim Turk from their wedding, 1957, Fukuoka, Japan. Michie on their honeymoon in Kyoto, Japan. Michie and Jim from their civil ceremony. Michie's Easter look in San Jose, CA.

Clockwise from top left: Trina and sister Lia in Easter outfits. Trina as a toddler in San Jose, CA. Jim Turk and his children, Lia, Trina, and Carter. Trina and her parents. Trina, Christmas Day 1965. Swimming in the backyard.

# introduction

I started Trina Turk twenty-five years ago, in May of 1995. It's been an entrepreneurial and creative adventure, a milestone best-celebrated visually. This is a story of color, print, optimism, and California.

After working as a designer for mostly junior companies for twelve years, I was under the mistaken impression that I knew everything you needed to know to launch an apparel company. My motivations were the same as those any creative entrepreneur has in mind when they decide to start their own business: working for yourself, not having a boss, being somewhat in control of your own destiny, more creative freedom, the challenge of "pulling it off," and establishing a successful business.

Although I'd love to say that the entire vision of a print-driven lifestyle brand inspired by California living was fully realized from the beginning, that was not the case. I really just wanted to create and produce my own collection. At thirty-four, it was the right time to give it a shot, to avoid regret later in life for never having tried. With minimal savings for funding, and no business plan, I just dove in and figured it out day by day, fueled by enthusiastic determination. It's apparent now that had there been an official business plan, it might have been daunting enough to discourage even beginning. In this case, naiveté was a bonus. If the fledgling company didn't succeed, at least I'd have a great portfolio that would enable a move into designing higher-end clothing.

In those early days, I was the sole employee, working out of a spare bedroom in our Los Feliz home. I designed there, and then drove all over Los Angeles, in my trusty '69 Karmann Ghia, with rolls of fabric, garments, trims, and patterns to collaborate with freelance patternmakers and sample sewers, focused on accomplishing whatever was necessary to get the first sample collection completed. After years of never wearing what I had designed at previous jobs, fashioning pieces in gorgeous fabrics that I actually wanted to wear was the objective. It was exciting and encouraging to receive orders from Saks Fifth Avenue, Barneys New York, and the influential Los Angeles shop Fred Segal with that first collection.

Inspiration has always come from classic American sportswear: the style of Audrey Hepburn, Doris Duke in her young, Hawaiian days, Ali MacGraw, Mary Tyler Moore, and Jackie O. Talitha Getty, and Elizabeth Taylor in their extravagant caftans were on my radar, as well as the graphic, modern style of Rudi Gernreich, Pierre Cardin, and Marimekko. Other American designers like Donald Brooks, Pauline Trigère, and Bonnie Cashin expressed that sophisticated simplicity I found appealing. Growing up in California and Washington in the '60s and '70s also came into play—two decades when vivid color was embraced enthusiastically in both fashion and interiors. The climate, landscape, architecture, and cross-cultural mix of Los Angeles were an ever-present backdrop and source of ideas. The diversity and creative energy of the city fed my constant craving for new ideas to meet the relentless deadlines of the industry.

Jonathan Skow, my late husband, and I, met in 1981 at the University of Washington in Seattle. He had successive majors—art, and then apparel design, eventually graduating with a marketing degree. We ended up in several classes together, including historic costume and textile science. He seemed an engaging character, clearly interested in his own unique style and not at all concerned about what others thought about him. In a life-figure drawing class, Jonathan only drew shoes.

The apparel-design program was quaint—it was a leftover from the home economics department, and had little to do with preparing for a real career. The U of W is a fine institution, but let's be honest, it was an obscure place to study fashion. Nonetheless, I earned a BA in apparel design there. Jonathan and I prioritized thrifting throughout the greater Seattle area, and concocting new-wave club looks to go out in, over studying during our college years. We loved examining the fabrics and construction of vintage garments, utilizing our newfound knowledge from textile and patternmaking classes.

I moved to Los Angeles to design for Ocean Pacific (OP), the surfwear company. Prints have always been an integral part of surf culture—think Hawaiian shirts and printed board shorts. In the course of designing OP juniors, I learned the technique of developing printed textiles. It was the mid-1980s, and multicolored, air-brushed, tropical florals were all the rage. We were still printing in Japan, and all the artwork was still done by hand. Working with prints and colorways became the best part of the job, noticing how hues play off each other, and how a feeling of movement could enhance a pattern.

Jonathan came to Los Angeles six months after my arrival here. We drove to Las Vegas one weekend and got married, and then continued thrift shopping; frequenting estate sales, flea markets, and antique shows; and perusing auction previews and catalogs. Our selections informed our personal style and decor, and it was an education in the designers, artists, brands, labels, and craftspeople who had created the items we preferred. It was a hobby we were passionate about, and it had more to do with our future business than we realized at the time.

At OP, we often purchased artwork from European design studios where textile designers created prints specifically geared to the apparel and home-furnishings markets, incorporating whatever the trends of the moment were. Viewing the studios' work was enlightening, but I recognized that the prints at the flea market were equally *au courant*. The treasure trove of patterns there was so appealing that Jonathan and I began collecting vintage prints in earnest, and as a side business had a sales rep selling them to the apparel industry. At that point, we collected any printed textile we thought was salable, but had a special affection for bold, colorful prints from the late '60s and early '70s, and amassed a large collection.

Jonathan's work as a freelance fashion stylist began taking him with increasing frequency to locations in and around Palm Springs. One of these was Jim Moore's 1962 steel-framed Wexler/Harrison House, which is a Palm Springs dream house: zigzag roofline, white terrazzo floors, walls of glass, and a beautiful aqua pool. As soon as we realized that an original-condition, mid-century, weekend home was within our reach, we joined the ranks of recreational real-estate shoppers and embarked upon a search for the perfect Palm Springs home.

We found the Ship of the Desert in 1998. The house was given the moniker in a 1937 *Sunset* magazine article in which it was featured on the cover. Trina Turk—the company—was three years old at the time. We had yet to turn any significant profit, but, somehow, we convinced ourselves that purchasing a weekend home that was larger, more expensive, and more of a wreck than what we had been looking for was a great idea.

It did turn out to be a great idea. We became immersed in the reemergence of Palm Springs. We went on architectural tours, shopped for vintage home furnishings, became members of the then-nascent Palm Springs Modern Committee, and met lots of design-oriented new friends. The iconic 1947 Richard Neutra-designed Kaufmann House had just been restored, and we were amused to find ourselves at the very house, which, as photographed by Slim Aarons, had inspired the lifestyle that we referenced in our clothing. We spent weekends enjoying warm, sunny weather, clean air, incredible natural beauty, a respite from city life, and cultural activities that were unexpected for a relatively small community. Travelers from all over the world were visiting, lured by the modernist architecture and the sun. Joshua Tree was nearby for a wilder, high-desert experience.

We talked about opening a retail store to serve these new residents of Palm Springs who were purchasing and restoring mid-century homes. It was our professional shopper's opinion that for clothing there was no appropriate retail in town to serve this demographic. Since our clothing was inspired by the "cocktails by the pool" lifestyle of Palm Springs, we imagined it would work.

We often stopped by John's Resale, where I always reminded Jonathan that, if this space ever became available, it should be our first boutique. At the time, we weren't aware that the building was designed by the acclaimed desert architect Albert Frey, but we were aware of the feeling of openness and light. Driving into town for Labor Day weekend 2001, there was a for-lease sign in the window. The lease was signed on September 10th. The next day was September 11th, 2001, which did not bode well for retail of any kind. But, having no idea what the ramifications of 9/11 actually were, we moved forward.

I admired the work of a Los Angeles-based interior designer—Kelly Wearstler—which I'd seen in the *Los Angeles Times* and other shelter

Clockwise from top left: At the beach in St. Augustine, FL. Trina modeling her college designs with friend Lisa Benko, 1983, Seattle, WA. Trina and Jonathan with their very first shipment of Trina Turk clothing in 1995, along with nephew Kima and niece Kalina. First house in Los Angeles, 1989. A Polaroid self portrait by Jonathan. On the road in Death Valley, CA.

Clockwise from top left: Jonathan at Santa Barbara airport. Jonathan shooting the summer 2017 collection. Trina at the Abernathy House, Palm Springs. Jonathan shooting in the pool at renowned architect Albert Frey's Frey House II in Palm Springs.

magazines, thinking that when it was time to do a store, she'd get it. She was finishing up what was then the Estrella Inn—now the Avalon—and was interested in the project. The brief for what we envisioned was a bright, airy version of the swanky feel of the interiors in '70s *Palm Springs Life* magazines. Our goal was to recreate a touch of the resort glamour of the old Bullock's, Robinson's, and the Palm Springs general store, which I've been told carried Pucci amidst hardware and sundries back in the day.

It was thrilling to display the collection in a fully designed environment. Seeing the boutique finished and merchandised was a gratifying moment. Kelly created a space that still feels fresh, although I silently curse her whenever we replace the white shag carpeting, which is often.

We have carried a bit of vintage clothing and furniture in the Palm Springs shop since we opened. The vintage menswear sold quickly, so we started to cut leftover rolls of prints into men's shirts, shorts, trousers, and jackets—but they still had a Trina Turk label. Our male clientele wholeheartedly embraced the color and pattern, but were miffed that the fresh deliveries of menswear were less generous and more erratic than the womenswear. Jonathan decided to fix the problem, and put his years of styling to use to design the menswear collection we dubbed Mr Turk. It's become a significant part of our business in Palm Springs, Los Angeles, New York, and Miami. The Mr Turk man is not a wallflower, and, in fact, is sometimes not a man. We sell the patterned jackets in particular to women, too, especially now, when the oversized jacket is on trend.

Meanwhile—from 1998–2001—Jonathan spent much of two and a half years in the desert working with Marmol Radziner as our house was fully restored after a devastating fire. Jonathan switched from fashion stylist to photographer during that time, and began shooting images for Trina Turk. The architectural tours prompted us to use many of these homes as photo shoot locations, which cemented the brand's association with Palm Springs.

Jonathan participated much more in the creation of our company's identity than just taking photos. He was a sounding board for any idea since the very beginning. His work as a stylist meant he was in the shops and costume houses constantly, and he made a point of relaying whatever inspired him. Referencing films, photography, art, fashion magazines, and TV shows was part of our language, with a free flow of influence back and forth. Jonathan always was more focused on the big picture and was never shy about sharing his opinion, which I respected and valued. He had great taste.

For the photo shoots themselves, he acted as the photographer and creative director, but could also be a prop stylist, set designer, location scout, or casting department—and was not above fluffing a pocket square, tying a scarf, dragging a piece of patio furniture across the beach, or demonstrating to the model exactly the body position or expression he wanted them to assume.

In the Spring of 2005, I dropped by the Parker Palm Springs hotel to see what was new in the reimagining of it. By chance, as I was introducing myself to someone at the front desk, Jonathan Adler popped out and asked me if I would like a tour. I was a fan of his work and his color sense, and loved the exuberant wackiness of the Parker's new decor.

Simultaneously, Jonathan Skow and I had been searching for a retail space in New York City. We had finally found a space on Gansevoort Street in the meatpacking district. It took forever to find something we liked, partly because we were spoiled by the sunny, warm spaces that are readily available in southern California but a rarity in New York City, at least in our price range. Since Jonathan Adler was based in New York, and we appreciated his decor at the Parker, we contacted him about designing the store. David Mann, of MR Architecture + Decor, was suggested as the project architect by Jonathan Adler, who focused on the interior design. We had coincidentally met David several years earlier on a Palm Springs Art Museum architectural tour. This time our inspiration was Big Sur and 1970s California arts and crafts, which we thought a good fit with a building from the 1880s.

While we were working on the New York store, which opened in December 2006, we had another project in the works in Los Angeles with Silverlake-based architect Barbara Bestor of Bestor Architecture. We were at the point where we needed a corporate showroom for wholesale sales. Prior to this, we had been represented by a multi-line showroom that showed other collections in addition to Trina Turk.

I became aware of Barbara's work much in the same way as Kelly's—noticing stories in various publications, and making a mental note for a future project. In Barbara's case it didn't hurt that her office was very near our house in Los Feliz, she was a modernist, and she clearly loved color. The idea of working with a woman who had her own architectural firm was intriguing. Over the years, we've worked together on two wholesale showrooms, four boutiques, and the restoration of a 1940s John Lautner-designed house in Echo Park in Los Angeles.

We now have eleven retail stores and three wholesale showrooms scattered across the country. Working with Kelly Wearstler, Jonathan Adler, Barbara Bestor, Phillip K. Smith III, David Mann of MR Architecture + Decor, Marmol Radziner, and their teams to create spaces—not to mention all of the amazing craftspeople who get the details done—has been an incredibly rewarding experience, although not something I thought about or anticipated. The tremendous knowledge gained from each project has informed whatever the next thing might be.

In 2018, Jonathan Skow died tragically as a result of an injury he suffered while body-surfing in Hawaii. It's been difficult in a way that's impossible to articulate to anyone who has not experienced a similar loss. As Nietzsche said, "That which does not kill us makes us stronger." I've really tried to focus on honoring his creativity to carry me through, and to remember the joy and enthusiasm we shared from the very beginning.

At the time of this writing, our flagship has been open for eighteen years in Palm Springs. We've expanded twice, and now occupy the entire Frey building. We've witnessed the revival of North Palm Canyon Drive—now called the Uptown Design District. What used to be a desolate strip has filled in with a lively assortment of shops and restaurants. A happily unintended consequence of our location has been the revitalization of the area.

Putting an outfit together is similar to putting a room together: you take into account body shape or architecture, and then mix colors, textures, and proportions to create a pleasing whole. It's a matter of composition, but on a different scale, with the connection between the two being the use of textiles. The relationship between fashion and interiors for the Trina Turk brand, as well as other categories, has always been our prints. Not all prints that work for a dress will work for an upholstered sofa or draperies, but with changes in scale and coloration, and a critical eye for what works, many can. There are patterns that we've run in everything from swim, to men's and women's apparel, to beach bags and home furnishings fabrics, that have resonated across the board. A great print is a great print, and people will respond to it.

After all this time, my favorite part of the process is still arranging the collage of fabrications, prints, colors, and textures, along with styling details and silhouettes, that create a collection. It's completely instinctive and always a search for that moment when one slight change makes it feel right. Established parameters and consistent touchstones certainly help. Palm Springs, the multi-culti sprawl of Los Angeles, car culture, surf culture, pop culture, modernist architecture, the art world, classic American sportswear and resort wear, graphic pattern, vivid color, and the optimistic indoor/outdoor lifestyle of California will continue to influence and lead the Trina Turk aesthetic into the future. It's hard to believe it's been twenty-five years.

**trina turk**

Clockwise from top left: Caftan party, Palm Springs. Jonathan at the John Lautner-designed Bob Hope house, Palm Springs. At home in Palm Springs. Sailing in Turkey.

# inspiration

A customary question posed to designers is "What inspires you?" The simple answer is that inspiration can come from anywhere. You never know what might spark an idea. A swatch of fabric, a color combination in nature, or a vintage photograph could be the seed of an entire collection. Perhaps it's something where the story already exists, as in a film, the work of an artist, a locale, or an era. Travel is always a fascinating visual feast, but home can be as well. The colors, landscape, climate, architecture, multi-cultural mix, and people that create the fabric of a dynamic twenty-first-century city like Los Angeles could inspire for years—and they have.

The following pages are a small sampling of the rich mélange of visuals that have initiated ideas: poolside in Palm Springs, Marbella, and Beverly Hills; mid-century modern architecture by luminaries Richard Neutra and Albert Frey; photography of these notable homes—with or without their stylish inhabitants—by revered photographers Slim Aarons and Julius Shulman; 1960s fashion by print-loving designers Pierre Cardin, Rudi Gernreich, and Emilio Pucci; and personal snapshots of travels and sights that have opened my mind and my eyes to art, beauty, and culture around the world.

# taste + style
## a conversation between simon doonan and trina turk

**simon:** Are you a fashion plate?

**trina:** I don't think of myself as a fashion plate. I love clothes, and have a lot of them (how could I not with eleven deliveries per year to choose from?), but I'm a practical gal, and am mostly concerned with being appropriately dressed for whatever is going on that day.

**simon:** I always look forward to seeing what you are wearing. You recently swung by our apartment in NYC wearing a TT silk printed top, black pants, accessorized with a massive vintage pendant, and a 1920s-inspired Givenchy (fake) fur, slung nonchalantly over the shoulders. Major! Let's talk about today's outfit.

**trina:** Today I'm California winter cozy. This pale camel heather batwing sweater is TT. I love the voluminous sleeves. I'm wearing one of my absolute favorite necklaces: Georg Jensen with these dangly rods that have a lovely hammered texture. Vintage 1970s sterling Scandinavian jewelry is definitely an obsession, and if it moves, that's even better.

I wear this Ann Dexter Jones silver ID bracelet almost every day, and the Betony O-ring ring is also in heavy rotation.

The jeans are a skinny, black, high-waisted style from Frame, with vaguely sailor-y button details, and silver, Fendi, block-heel, Chelsea boots. The elastic panel on the sides has a stitched texture like a tiny fisherman sweater with mini tipping stripes—a refined reference to a tube sock. I threw a black Marni zip poncho over the whole thing this morning—you can't wear batwing sleeves with a normal jacket.

**simon:** When It comes to your style, you always appear bold and confident. Is your personal style instinctive? Or is this an illusion? Maybe you lay awake at night obsessing about your look for the next day?

**trina:** My personal style is inherited from my Japanese mom, and selective nature from my Dad. Michie Sugimoto Turk loves a fully accessorized head-to-toe look, even at age ninety. Jim Turk (aka Diego) is extremely discriminating about colors, textures, and weights of what he wears.

If I lay awake at night, it's not about my look for the next day. I don't plan looks ahead unless it's for an event, or a trip with a particular climate. I'm not above theme dressing—in fact, a theme is so great for setting the tone—I wish all events had themes.

For a regular work week, I never plan what I'm wearing in advance, sometimes resulting in a pile of options left on the floor and running a tad late. If I wear something I'm not fully on board with, I'll feel slightly unsettled and usually end up rummaging for a fresh option in the vintage room.

**simon:** I remember a party where you were wearing an incredible sweeping Lanvin dress in apricot, and somebody dumped a glass of red wine over it. The next day you went and bought the exact same dress to replace it. What does that say about you?

**trina:** Oh my god; I love that dress! It's a one-shoulder silk gazar number with a big pouf of fabric that sits on your shoulder from the Alber Elbaz era. By the way, the dress is actually brilliant orange, not apricot.

What it says about me is that I will go to extreme lengths to find a particular item if necessary. In this case I had to wear that dress again—one cocktail party was not enough. It was apparently pre-Instagram ... The store in London was the only shop that still had another, so they sent it.

**simon:** I was in your Palm Springs house, and I needed to tinkle. I opened the wrong door and—kapow!—I found myself staring into your caftan closet. #color #drama #dazzle #peggyguggenheim #mrsroper #liberace. Talk to me about caftans.

**trina:** So *you're* the person who tinkled in my caftan closet. I thought it was Frances, a friend's Frenchie. Caftans are just the thing to wear in Palm Springs, which is why my collection is housed there. They're perfect poolside with a cocktail, or over your maillot if you've actually done some swimming. They look equally chic barefoot, with flats, or with a metallic heel.

That sweep of fabric lends an air of airy elegance, whether printed, solid, striped, embellished, or whatever. With Mrs. Roper, it was the hair, makeup, and voice that made it funny ...

I've amassed quite an array over the years: tie-dyes from Rwanda, block prints from India, vintage Hawaiiana, Pucci extravaganzas, soutache trim from Morocco, crinkle viscose with lurex from Greece, and, of course, a myriad of TT patterns. At Trina Turk HQ, we've abandoned casual Friday for caftan Friday if it's eighty degrees or over.

**simon:** I remember when you started designing swimwear. I was skeptical. The margins are great, but it's such a tricky business, and women hate nothing more than trying on swimwear. How have you managed to build such a mega-groovy swimwear brand?

**trina:** I've been excited about swim since our above-ground backyard pool in 1960s San Jose suburbia was installed! Growing up in California, I spent many weekends at the beach, and that sensibility sunk in. The glamorous resort stories in vintage fashion mags are favorites: Veruschka splashing in Brazilian waves; elegant Louise Dahl-Wolfe images of models posing next to an arched colonnade or latticework screens in Tunisia; Dovima oiled up and stretched out in polka dots (the first bikini in *Harper's Bazaar*); impossibly leggy Marie Helvin shot by David Bailey in silver or orchid against a background of aqua swimming pool; the Deborah Turbeville photos of artfully arranged models in a bathhouse; and, naturally, all of the Slim Aarons photos of chic people in chic locales baking in the sun.

Swimwear was an organic addition since it's always been color- and print-centric. The established association with California and Palm Springs didn't hurt—and added sexiness and furthered our storyline of "California Chic."

In the early days of our swim collection, we developed jewelry-like hardware accents that, along with our signature prints, became part of our swimwear lexicon. Fit is incredibly important, and we've developed a fit that's sexy but wearable—no worries about bits popping out!

**simon:** I also want to know how you tweak those oversized prints so that they work on itsy-bitsy bikinis.

**trina:** Our Pisces or Peacock Ikat prints have made appearances in both our indoor/outdoor home furnishings fabric collection as well as on a bikini—but the scale has to be adapted to fit the end use. We always hold patterns against the body before making decisions, since it might look great flat on a table, but on the body it can be flattering—or not.

For swim, we often work with templates that are cut out in the shape of a bikini or a one-piece, and move them across the print, looking for the perfect placement. We do many engineered, specifically placed prints so what you see is what you get, and there is no variation from one garment to another.

**simon:** Speaking of the ocean: I remember once when we were in Capri you said you loved the color combo of the coral, juxtaposed with the turquoise water. Did you ever incorporate that color combo into a collection?

**trina:** Oh yes—turquoise plus coral is a perennial TT favorite, even better with a splash of limoncello yellow. Capri is so full of color inspo! The blue-and-white-striped beach umbrellas, the trees loaded with oranges, the bougainvillea in every hue ...

Travel is a real eye opener when it comes to ideas for color palettes and pairings. Mexico, Turkey, and India are the most colorful places I've visited—swoon-worthy textiles and patterns everywhere. In Portugal and Morocco, it's about the tiles—designs from baroque to mod in Portugal; and classic geos, stars, and zigzags in Morocco. In Japan, the vermillion red, black, and gold of lacquerware lends itself to colorations that have been incorporated into holiday collections. As Diana Vreeland said, "The eye has to travel."

Left to right: Jonathan Skow, Jonathan Adler, Simon Doonan, and Trina Turk in Capri, Italy

**simon:** Not only are you a brilliant designer, you are also a brilliant shopper, a connoisseur. When did your shopping odyssey begin?

**trina:** My earliest shopping odyssey began when I accompanied my mom to the fabric store in grade school. She allowed me to select patterns and styles for my back-to-school wardrobe, which she then expertly whipped up on her home sewing machine. Things really got rolling in the early 1980s when my new college friend Jonathan (later my husband) and I spent countless hours in the Goodwills, Value Villages, and Salvation Army stores of the greater Seattle area. It was a time when you could still find 1940s, nipped-waist, shoulder-padded jackets; Harris tweed overcoats; 1950s fit-and-flare dresses; cool men's neckties for 50 cents; all beautifully constructed and in gorgeous fabrics.

When we moved to Los Angeles in 1985, we discovered there was a flea market every weekend and became addicted to the thrill of the hunt almost every Sunday morning. We frequented the Rose Bowl, Long Beach, and Pasadena City College markets, and furnished our Park La Brea apartment and ourselves with vintage flair.

**simon:** Along with Anna Wintour, Ziggy Stardust, Elvis, and Edith Head, you have an iconic hairdo. Tell me about your hair journey.

**trina:** My half-Japanese hair likes to do one thing: it hangs straight. As a little kid, I had long and short bob variations with some pixie cuts thrown in. In the '70s, I wore my hair long, straight, and parted in the middle, just like everyone else. I tried the Dorothy Hamill wedge and a sleek mushroom-cap style in junior high. I permed it in high school attempting an *au courant* triangular silhouette—it was 1978—but it didn't really take. In college, I cut it short, seeking a new-wave look. That evolved to a full-on crewcut, which caused me to be mistaken for a gentleman when flying to Asia for work in the early '80s—the big shoulder pads and heavy, black-framed men's glasses probably didn't help. After moving to Los Angeles in 1985 (and growing out the crewcut), I wore it pulled back into a ponytail tied with a scarf for a few years. Then I settled on a bob, and have had variations of them ever since: short and Buster Brown-ish; shoulder-length and choppy; bangs; no bangs; currently with a lot of texture, sans hard edges.

**simon:** Your interest in fashion seems to run parallel with your interest in architecture. How do these two passions coexist in your life?

**trina:** It's all one big design project as far as I'm concerned.

I love an architectural tour. The era doesn't matter since each style informs the others, and it's the compare and contrast that's fascinating. Jonathan and I always loved the character and detail of old buildings. When we moved to Los Angeles, we started going on architectural tours regularly, and realized that we loved architecture as much as clothing. We discovered the treasure trove of mid-century architecture in both Los Angeles and Palm Springs.

Our homes progressed from cute stucco bungalow, to red-tile-roofed Spanish Colonial Revival, to modern all the way. I'm a believer that living and working in a well-designed (and well-decorated!) space enhances your well-being and creativity.

**simon:** Your taste and your style have evolved in dialogue with Jonathan, your fabulous husband, who is dearly missed. RIP. Now you are obliged to continue your aesthetic journey solo. This cannot be easy.

**trina:** Sigh. It's been almost a year and a half since Jonathan died, and the ramifications of his absence manifest daily. We met in our early twenties, grew up together, honed our tastes together, traveled the world together, watched trends come and go, and collaborated. Although I realize I'm fortunate to have had thirty-seven years of adventures with a person who exuded joie de vivre, and a creative partnership that went beyond business to fashioning all aspects of how we lived, sadly, that's my old life. The optimistic outlook would be, "It's a new chapter," or new beginning. He wanted me to live life to the fullest, so I'm trying my best.

**simon:** Thanks for sharing … and Cher-ing.

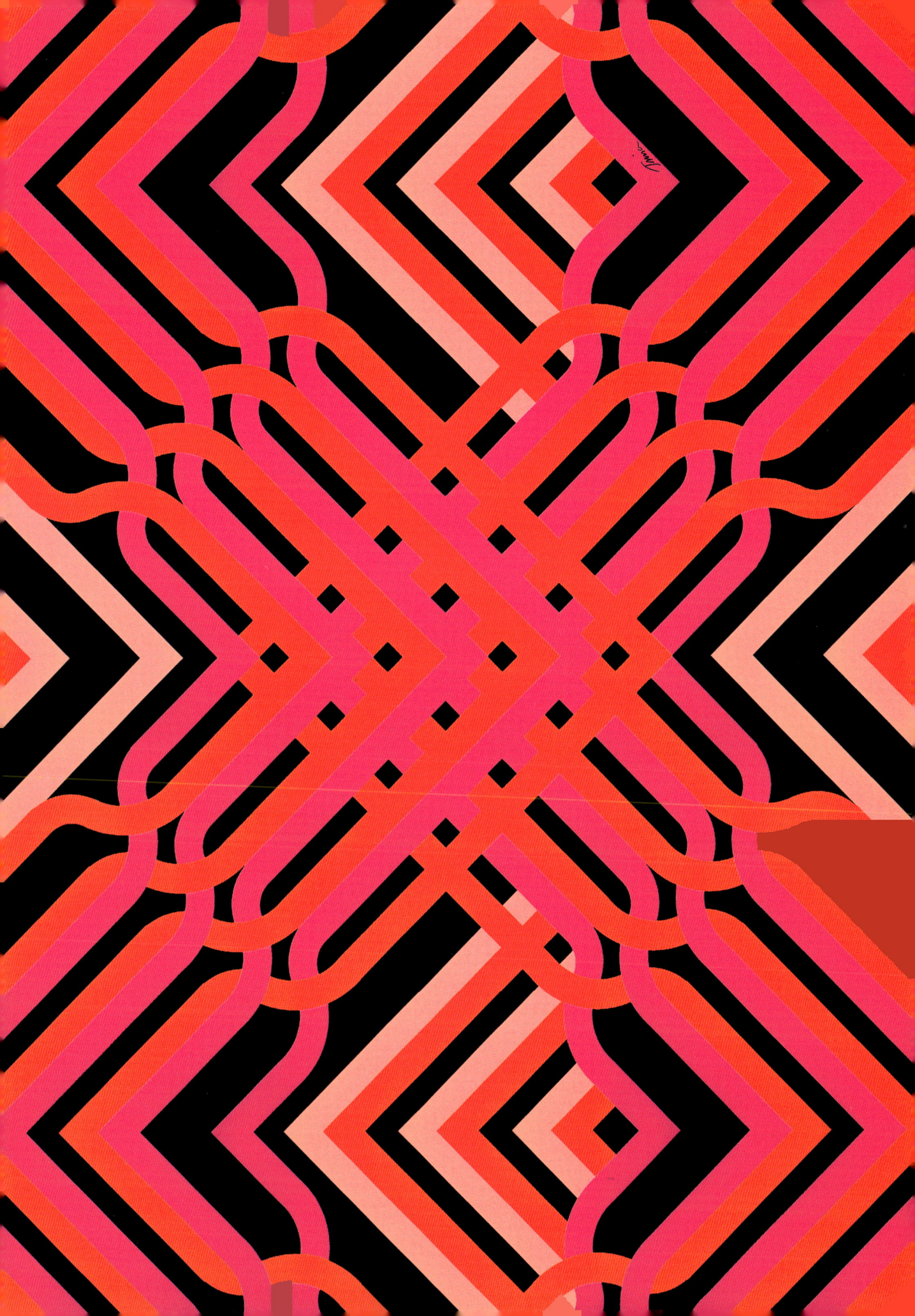

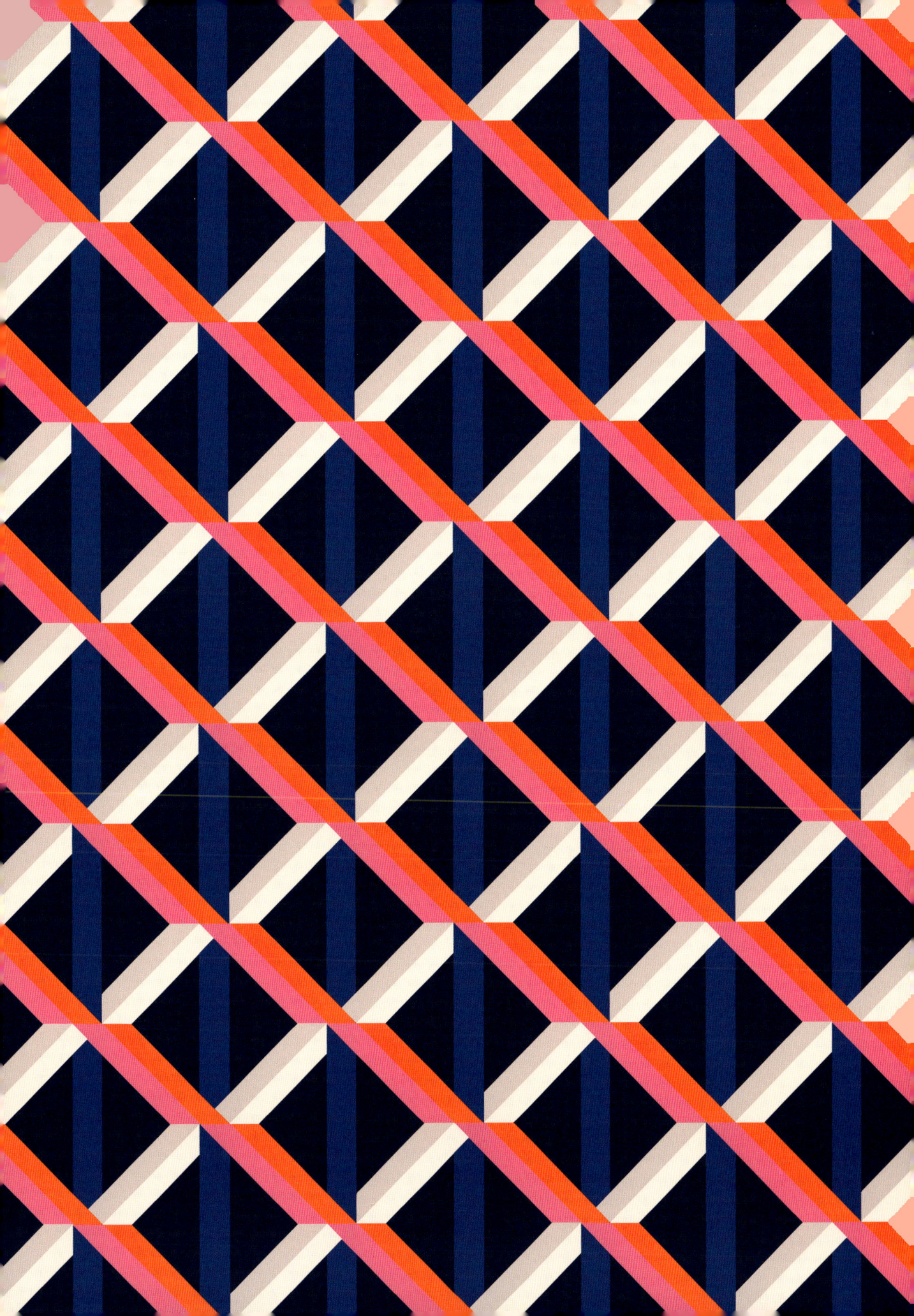

# environments

There is something about the natural environment of beaches and deserts—the sandy neutral palette, the emphasis on bodies at play, that is the perfect setting for the riotous and pleasurable explosion of color and pattern that makes up the Trina Turk and Mr Turk brand. Whether you are poolside in Palm Springs, cliff walking at Sea Ranch or surfing in Huntington Beach (or FEEL like being transported to any of the above) there is a bigger idea about design and architecture for lifestyle that permeates Trina's world. California has been a strong source of innovation and experimentation in American design and architecture for the last century, and Trina Turk has created a powerful language for expressing that creativity through fashion. What is not as well known is her impact via her building and preservation of modern environments. When I first started working with Trina we did a panel together for Palm Springs Modernism Week and she memorably said that for her, "Modernism is Optimism." I think that perfectly frames her approach to environments, whether her own living spaces, her stores, headquarters and even her incredibly glamorous and unique research destinations (Morocco! Mallorca! India! Brazil! Hawaii!). The anthropological magpie-shopper gene that she shares with Charles and Ray Eames has led to extensive travel and collecting of objects that comes back into new collections, patterns and ideas. At the same time in and around California she and Jonathan collected a remarkable group of architectural landmark houses from the 1930s to the 1960s. They restored each precious gem and happily lived in them and those houses often provided the backdrop for the brand's photo shoots. Perhaps inspired by the amazing photography of Slim Aarons, who within his images would seamlessly integrate new architecture, like Neutra's Kaufmann House in Palm Springs, with the documenting of fabulous people (who also lived there!) having a great time and looking glamorous. This lifestyle imagery is part of a lived reality rather than an advertising image—it is art as life!

Trina has made art, commerce and lifestyle all part of an optimistic modernist continuum. From her Palm Springs store nestled within an Albert Frey building, to restoring the "Lost Lautner" in Echo Park to her latest acquisition—Joseph Esherick's own hedgerow house at Sea Ranch—there is a thru-line of stewardship. She finds these new strands of modernist DNA that need a care taker and she then brings them back to life to play a role in the vibrancy of contemporary design and lifestyle. I am not sure how many awards for preserving modernism Trina has won, but it is an awful lot—there really is not anyone else in California doing this work and generously giving back to the institutions that help preserve and promote modern art and culture.

I see several strands of non-architectural design history playing a part in the bigger story of Trina's unique California Modernism: from Alexander Girard, Emilio Pucci, Deborah Sussman, Saul Bass, Jim Isermann to many others. The very *au courant* mode of her work involves creating something completely new while synthesizing a collection of influences from what has come before.

## barbara bestor

# los angeles showroom
### design by barbara bestor

The Cooper Design Space has been integral to downtown Los Angeles' apparel industry for decades. Working with Bestor Architecture, the showroom design focuses on a simple palette of materials: wood, white laminate, mirrors, and glass, with pops of color provided by the clothing collection and furnishings. We softened up the industrial feel of a concrete floor and exposed ductwork with a pair of 1970s Romeo Reyna textile art pieces; hot pink carpeting; a platform-style, custom seating area topped by multicolored silk tussah pillows; placed plywood wall panels; and marble-topped Saarinen tables with Gio Ponti spindle-back chairs.

# palm springs boutique
### architecture by albert frey, original interiors by kelly wearstler, subsequent design by barbara bestor

Our first boutique opened in 2002 in a building designed by Albert Frey. Optimism permeates the space, starting with the wall of plate glass windows along Palm Canyon Drive. Kelly Wearstler created the original interior design. Two subsequent expansions were designed by Phillip K. Smith III in 2008, and Bestor Architecture in 2012. Embracing the sunny desert ambience to create a light-filled space was constant through each new iteration. The shop extended from the initial women's collection storefront to include mini-departments for year-round swimwear, limited edition Mr Turk menswear, and Trina Turk Residential—decorative accessories, an array of gifts, and books to inspire.

# third street boutique
### design by kelly wearstler

"It's like being in a glass of pink champagne." The brief for our first boutique in Los Angeles was to create a modern take on the elegant old-school Bullocks Wilshire department store salon. Kelly Wearstler divided the thirty-three-hundred-square-foot building into three lounge-like areas with pink-tiled floors, ogee screens over rose gold mirrors, blush moiré wallpaper, alcoves housing the collection, and the bubbly sensation of eighty glass globes hung at varying heights from the ceiling. The forty-foot glass façade of the former feather trim factory affords a glimpse inside even when driving by.

# new york boutique
### design by jonathan adler in collaboration with MR architecture + decor

A burst of color in the Meatpacking District, Trina Turk New York opened in 2006 in a historic 1880s building. Admiration for Jonathan Adler's work at the Parker Palm Springs Hotel made his uninhibited style a perfect match for the "1970s Big Sur" vision for the shop. The collaborative effort resulted in white textures layered with splashes of color. Elements throughout are chic yet crafty, including a macramé room divider, ceramic tile created by Adler, sunburst-carved doors, and a smattering of vintage and Jonathan Adler furnishings amongst white-painted pecky cypress walls, brass hardware, and brightly hued silk tussah wall panels.

# bal harbour boutique
### design by MR architecture + decor

Miami's abundance of over-the-top architecture, swaying palm trees, azure skies, and long stretches of white sand beach conjures the dreamy resort fantasies of decades past. The flamboyant, fantastic hotels of Miami Modern architect Morris Lapidus and the palette of the sea, sky, and lush vegetation inspired the design of this shop, created by MR Architecture + Decor in 2009. We embraced curvy shapes, backlit ceiling coves, turquoise and white terrazzo, splashes of apple green and aqua, shelving embedded in breeze-block panels, and a touch of exoticism in an arched banquette seating area swagged with linen.

… # larchmont boutique
### design by barbara bestor

We collaborated again with Bestor Architecture for this shop on the main street of Los Angeles' Hancock Park neighborhood. Focusing on creating a modern, neutral backdrop for our vibrant print and pattern, we selected white oak and ivory silk tussah walls, curvilinear fixtures, arched doorways, and a custom brass reception desk that floats in the center of scalloped floor tile. A 1970s Lightolier chandelier adds a touch of vintage flair, with accents of sunshine yellow and turquoise appearing in the dressing rooms.

# ship of the desert palm springs
## webster and wilson architects, 1936. restoration by marmol radziner

After searching for a weekend home in the desert off and on for a couple of years, we knew this house was it the moment we walked in. It's a classic example of Streamline Moderne style, beautifully sited against the San Jacinto mountains. We were taken by its gracious scale, the view of the valley, and its embrace of the outdoors, with a deck or patio off almost every room. We steered clear of nautical references when decorating, beginning with a neutral palette that has evolved over the years, incorporating color in addition to a myriad of objects and furnishings from decades of collecting.

# schapiro house los feliz
## j.r. davidson architect, 1949

When Jonathan was working as a stylist, he would occasionally come home and recount in great detail a particular mid-century house that was the location for the day. He worked there now and then, and would rave about it every time. Jonathan was out of town when our realtor showed me a place that fit the description of what we were looking for. It had been thoroughly described to me so many times that when I walked in, I realized it was the location house. We, and now I, have lived there since 2002, with the mostly vintage decor becoming more layered, and the landscaping lusher over time. It's a quintessential example of California mid-century post and beam architecture emphasizing indoor/outdoor living.

# salkin house echo park
## john lautner architect, 1948. restoration by barbara bestor

Architect John Lautner hadn't yet received his license at the time of permitting for the Salkin House, one of the reasons it had mysteriously dropped off the radar of architecture enthusiasts. Additions had obscured the dramatic shape of the house, and it had fallen into disrepair after having been rented for decades. Billed the "Long Lost Lautner" when it came onto the market in 2015, Jonathan and I saw it as an incredible opportunity to restore a little gem. Others saw it as a teardown—it was in terrible shape. Progress was slow but exciting as we saw the assertive original design re-emerge. Bestor Architecture resolved the leakage issues that had plagued the house with solutions not available in 1948. The original redwood paneling was in amazingly good condition, and came back to life with refinishing. We decorated the house in a bohemian style, finally finding a home for many pieces of vintage furniture, carpets purchased in Istanbul and Morocco, and artwork that had been in storage.

# esherick house sea ranch
## joseph esherick architect, 1966.

The Sea Ranch is an architectural community on the Sonoma Coast, about one hundred miles north of San Francisco. We first visited as weekend renters, and were enthralled by the juxtaposition of miles of trails, dramatic coastline, tide-pool beaches, serene meadows, cypress hedgerows, and a particular style of California modernist architecture based on the sheep barn vernacular of the area's past. We had no intention of buying there, until the house that founding Sea Ranch architect Joseph Esherick built for his own family became available. At a compact eight hundred fifty square feet, the house somehow incorporates three bedrooms, two bathrooms, and a spaciousness that belies its small size. The main level is cozily wedged into the meadow, with windows just above the level of the grass. The house spirals upwards from there, with a room or two on each level, and precisely placed windows offering angled light and postcard views.

# thank you

It takes a team to build a business, so thanks to all the Trina Turk team members past and present who have been vital to creating a company and a brand from humble beginnings. Thanks also to our freelance photo shoot team whose work is on display here in Jonathan's photos.

Thank you to all of our customers who have embraced color, print, and optimism for twenty-five years.

Thanks for your support in the early days:
Estevan Ramos started his own company and inspired me to start mine.
Laurie Hasson, Jeff Cohan, and Peter Berta were bold enough to take a chance on representing a designer who lacked experience in running or building a company, and convinced store buyers to place orders.
John Eshaya, who bought the first collection for Fred Segal.
Bert Forma, Danny Sassower, and several other fabric reps were so kind and helpful despite the very small orders.
Barry Cohn taught me what a factor was.
Ilse Metcheck of the CFA has been a cheerleader since the beginning.
Mary Chu's company has sewn our garments right here in Los Angeles for twenty-four years.

I had been talking about doing a book for years, so I was thrilled when Gloria Fowler and Steve Crist from Chronicle Chroma contacted me with the same idea. Gloria revealed the process of creating a book step by step and was gentle in her nudging as the deadlines approached. Thanks Gloria; it's been a pleasure working with you.

Thanks to Booth Moore, Simon Doonan, and Barbara Bestor for your contributions.

Thanks to Mallory Farrugia, who was unfazed as we added more and more images to the project. Jessica Jang was intrepid in finding those high-res files from photo shoots of years past. Thanks to Carol Meadows for keeping me somewhat organized, and to my sister Lia for proofreading and suggestions.

Thanks to my mom, Michie, for teaching me to sew, and demonstrating what style and attention to detail is all about. Thanks to my Dad, Jim, for instilling an appreciation of the beauty of California and the written word. Thank you Los Angeles, my home since 1985, and Palm Springs for all the sunny weekends.

Thank you Jonathan Skow, wherever you are, for thirty-seven years of creative adventures.

front and back covers: Trina Turk 25th Anniversary sunrise ombre floral print

     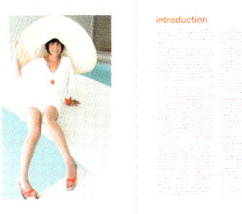

page 6 clockwise from top left: Jim Turk and Michie Sugimoto Turk wedding in Fukuoka, Japan, 1957. Michie on their honeymoon in Kyoto, Japan. Michie and Jim, civil ceremony in Fukuoka, Japan, 1957. Michie's Easter look in San Jose, CA
page 7: Turk family including Michie, Jim, Lia, Trina, and Carter

pages 8–9: Spring 2020 sunburst print

page 10: Trina at the Bolero House, Palm Springs, 2008. Photo by Jonathan Skow

    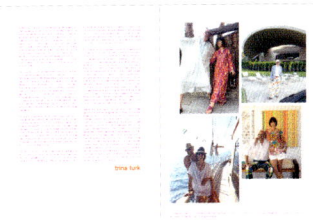 

page 13 clockwise from top left: St. Augustine, FL. Lisa Benko and Trina modeling college design school fashions in Seattle, WA, 1983. With nephew Kima and niece Kalina and cartons containing first Trina Turk shipments in Burlingame, CA, 1995. Our first house in Los Angeles, CA, 1989. Jonathan, Polaroid self-portrait, early 90s. Someone else's trailer as a prop in Death Valley, CA, 1986

page 14, clockwise from top left: Jonathan at the Santa Barbara airport, 2009, photo by John Lennon. Shooting the Summer 2017 collection in Palm Springs, CA, photo by Trina. Trina at the Abernathy House in Palm Springs, CA, photo by Jonathan Skow. Jonathan shooting in the pool at the Albert Frey-designed Frey II House in Palm Springs, CA, photo by Trina

page 17, clockwise from top left: Caftan party in Palm Springs, CA, 2018, photo by Eddie Scachnow. Jonathan at the John Lautner-designed Bob Hope House in Palm Springs, CA, 2008, photo by Trina. Coral von Zumwalt for Martha Stewart Living in Palm Springs, CA, 2009. Sailing on a gulet in Bodrum, Turkey

pages 18–19: Summer 2018 Lotus Flower print

page 21: Spring 2012 Pisces print strapless dress at the Richard Neutra-designed Kaufmann House in Palm Springs, CA. Photo by Carter Smith

page 22: Rippled blue toga over pink taffeta pants by Bill Blass, 1965. Photo by Horst P. Horst
page 23: Samantha Jones in a caftan set by Ken Scott in Rajasthan, India, 1967. Photo by Henry Clarke

pages 24–25: Party at the Kaufmann House in Palm Springs, CA, 1970. Photo by Slim Aarons

page 26: Pucci ensemble in Rajasthan, India, 1965. Photo by Henry Clarke
page 27: Veruschka in a voile jumpsuit in Barbados, 1965. Photo by Louis Faurer

page 28: Woman by the Pool, Beverly Hills Hotel, 1975. Photo by Anthony Friedkin

page 31: Peggy Moffitt wearing Rudi Gernreich, 1966. Photo by William Claxton

page 30: Moira Swan in Dior, 1969. Photo by Bert Stern

page 31: Samantha Jones in a zig zag print caftan by Livio de Simone in Udaipur, India, 1967. Photo by Henry Clarke

pages 32–33: Inspiration and travel photos from around the world including: Coachella, CA; Taormina, Italy; Antelope Valley, CA; Los Angeles, CA; Capri, Italy; Guadalajara, Mexico; Slot Canyons, UT; Palm Springs, CA; The Sea Ranch, CA; Shangri-La, Honolulu, HI; Bali, Indonesia; Kyoto, Japan; Amsterdam, The Netherlands; Tangier, Morocco; Havana, Cuba; Kyoto, Japan

pages 34–35: "Pool at El Venerol," Marbella, Spain, 1967. Photo by Slim Aarons

pages 36–37: Inspiration and travel photos from around the world including: The Alhambra, Granada, Spain; Aveiro, Portugal; Havana, Cuba; The Sea Ranch, CA; Capri, Italy; Paris, France; Tangier, Morocco; Coachella, CA; Palm Springs, CA; Guadalajara, Mexico; Arcosanti, AZ; Tokyo, Japan; Kauai, HI

pages 38–39: Albert Frey-designed Burgess House in Palm Springs, CA, 1984. Photo by Julius Schulman, copyright J. Paul Getty Trust. Getty Research Institute, Los Angeles (2004.R.10)

pages 40–41: Collage of Trina Turk and vintage jewelry and sunglasses. Photo by Nicole LaMotte

pages 42–43: Summer 2012 Las Flores print

page 44: Trina at the John Lautner-designed Lautner Compound in Desert Hot Springs, CA, 2013. Photo by Jonathan Skow

page 46: Jonathan Skow, Jonathan Adler, Simon Doonan, and Trina Turk sailing in Capri, Italy, 2009

pages 48–49: Summer 2017 Ginko print

pages 50–51: Resort 2016 "Hawaii 5-0" collection Theodora Caftan in Lehua print at the William Holden Estate in Palm Springs, CA, 2016. Photo by Jonathan Skow

page 52: Fall 2017 Joceline dress in Dahlia Dell print at the John Lautner-designed Salkin House in Echo Park, Los Angeles, CA. Photo by Jonathan Skow

page 53: Resort 2014 at the Craig Ellwood-designed Palevsky House in Palm Springs, CA. Photo by Jonathan Skow

pages 54–55: Summer 2017 "Vista Las Palmas" collection, Arboretum dress at a William Cody-designed house in Vista Las Palmas, Palm Springs, CA. Photo by Jonathan Skow

pages 56 and 57: Summer 2017 "Vista Las Palmas" collection, Ginko leaf top and chambray wrap pant at a William Cody-designed house in Vista Las Palmas, Palm Springs, CA. Photos by Jonathan Skow

pages 58 and 59: Resort 2014 at the Craig Ellwood-designed Palevsky House in Palm Springs, CA. Photos by Jonathan Skow

page 60, left: Spring 2014 in Carpinteria, CA. Photo by Jonathan Skow
page 60, right: Fall 2012 at the Los Angeles County Museum of Art, CA. Photo by Jonathan Skow
page 61: Spring 2014 in Carpinteria, CA. Photo by Jonathan Skow

pages 62 and 63: Spring 2008 at the Bolero House in Palm Springs, CA. Photos by Jonathan Skow

pages 64–65: Summer 2017 "Vista Las Palmas" collection at the James McNaughton-designed Villa Grigio in the Movie Colony, Palm Springs, CA. Photo by Jonathan Skow

pages 66 and 67: Spring 2011 "Palm Springs Eternal" collection in Palm Springs, CA. Photos by Jonathan Skow

page 68: Fall 2014 at the Richard Neutra-designed VDL House in Silverlake, Los Angeles, CA. Photo by Jonathan Skow
page 69: Fall 2013 at the John Lautner-designed Lautner Compound in Desert Hot Springs, CA. Photo by Jonathan Skow

page 70: Fall 2017 at the John Lautner-designed Salkin House in Echo Park, Los Angeles, CA. Photo by Jonathan Skow
page 71: Fall 2014 at the Richard Neutra-designed VDL House in Silverlake, Los Angeles, CA. Photo by Jonathan Skow

page 72: Resort 2005 in Malibu, CA. Photo by Jonathan Skow
page 73: Fall 2011 at the Flight Path Museum in Los Angeles, CA. Photo by Jonathan Skow

pages 74–75: Spring 2018 "Superbloom" collection at Garfield Park in South Pasadena, CA. Photo by Jonathan Skow

pages 76 and 77: Spring 2020 "Made in the Shade" collection at Oxnard Beach Park in Oxnard, CA. Photos by Dewey Nicks

pages 78 and 79: Spring 2020 25th Anniversary collection at Oxnard Beach Park in Oxnard, CA. Photos by Dewey Nicks

pages 80 and 81: Spring 2020 "Made in the Shade" collection at Oxnard Beach Park in Oxnard, CA. Photos by Dewey Nicks

pages 82–83: Fall 2018 at the Hearst House in Little Tuscany, Palm Springs, CA. Photo by Jonathan Skow

page 84: Spring 2015 "Flower Mart" collection in Alhambra, CA. Photo by Jonathan Skow
page 85: Residential rug and pillows with cabanas in Trina Turk Indoor/Outdoor for Schumacher Peacock Ikat print at the El Mirage dry lake bed, CA, 2010. Photo by Jonathan Skow

pages 86–87: Spring 2014 "Cali Road Trip" collection at the Albert Frey-designed Frey II House in Palm Springs, CA. Photo by Jonathan Skow

pages 88–89: Summer 2018 "California Dreaming" collection at Leo Carrillo State Beach in Malibu, CA. Photo by Jonathan Skow

pages 90–91: Spring 2014 towels at the Albert Frey-designed Frey II House in Palm Springs, CA. Photo by Jonathan Skow

page 92: Summer 2016 "Summer of Love" collection in Malibu, CA. Photo by Jonathan Skow
page 93: Summer 2005 in Malibu, CA. Photo by Jonathan Skow

pages 94 and 95: Poppy Print everything from the Spring 2015 "Flower Mart" collection in Alhambra, CA. Photos by Jonathan Skow

page 96: Spring 2014 "Cali Road Trip" collection in Carpinteria, CA. Photo by Jonathan Skow
page 97: Spring 2019 "The Tourist" collection on the Queen Mary in Long Beach, CA. Photo by Jonathan Skow

pages 98 and 99: Paddle board and surfboard collaboration with Walden Surfboards incorporating the Malibu Gold print, summer 2013. Photos by Jonathan Skow

page 100, left: Spring 2008 in Palm Springs, CA. Photo by Jonathan Skow
page 100, right: Spring 2010 in Chatsworth, CA. Photo by Jonathan Skow
page 101: Spring 2011 Trina Turk Residential pillows in Jonathan's vintage golf cart, Palm Springs, CA. Photo by Jonathan Skow

page 102: Spring 2011 "Palm Springs Eternal" collection in Malibu, CA. Photo by Jonathan Skow
page 103: Spring 2019 "The Tourist" collection on the Queen Mary in Long Beach, CA. Photo by Jonathan Skow

page 104: Spring 2008 Trina Turk Swim launch collection at the Bolero House in Palm Springs, CA. Photo by Jonathan Skow
page 105: Summer 2005 Chinoiserie Floral at the Parker Hotel in Palm Springs, CA. Photo by Jonathan Skow

page 106: Spring 2007 Supercharm print, Hollywood Hills, CA. Photo by Jonathan Skow
page 107: Trina Turk Residential embroidered pillows at the Craig Ellwood-designed Palevsky house in Palm Springs, CA. Photo by Jonathan Skow

page 108: Spring 2013 "Surf & Racquet Club" collection in Malibu, CA. Photo by Jonathan Skow
page 109: Resort 2010, Modern Drops print in downtown Los Angeles, CA. Photo by Jonathan Skow

page 110: Spring 2011, "Palm Springs Eternal" collection in Palm Springs, CA. Photo by Jonathan Skow
page 111: Spring 2011, "Palm Springs Eternal" collection at the Donald Wexler-designed Steel House, Racquet Club Estates, Palm Springs, CA. Photo by Jonathan Skow

page 112, left: Spring 2018 "Superbloom" collection, Garfield Park, South Pasadena, CA. Photo by Jonathan Skow
page 112, right: Pincushion protea, Big Sur, CA 2010. Photo by Jonathan Skow
page 113, left: Billy balls, Los Angeles, CA 2005. Photo by Jonathan Skow
page 113, right: Spring 2018 "Superbloom" collection, Garfield Park, South Pasadena, CA. Photo by Jonathan Skow

page 114: Spring 2014 "Cali Road Trip" collection in Carpenteria, CA. Photo by Jonathan Skow
page 115: Spring 2015 "Flower Mart" collection in Alhambra, CA. Photo by Jonathan Skow

page 116: Resort 2013 at the Charles Arnoldi Studio in Venice, CA. Photo by Jonathan Skow
page 117: Spring 2019, "The Tourist" collection on the Queen Mary in Long Beach, CA. Photo by Jonathan Skow

page 118: Holiday 2012 at the El Mirage dry lake bed, CA. Photo by Jonathan Skow
page 119: Holiday 2011 on the Queen Mary in Long Beach, CA. Photo by Jonathan Skow

pages 120–121: Summer 2017 Vivid Vista print

page 122: Spring 2018 Superbloom Stripe print
page 123: Summer 2018 Brasilia Collage print

page 124: Summer 2008 Paradise Tapestry print
page 125: Summer 2018 Day Dream Floral print

page 126: Holiday 2016 Cabaret Geo print
page 127: Resort 2020 Flying Cranes print

page 128: Spring 2021 "Florida Keys" collection, Island Swirl print
page 129: Fall 2015 Union Square Geo print

page 130: Spring 2021 "Florida Keys" collection, Going Your Way Chevron print
page 131: Spring 2017 Pop Art Heart print

page 132: Summer 2018 Day Dream Floral print
page 133: Resort 2015 "Baja" collection, Avenida Diamonds print

page 134: Spring 2019 "The Tourist" collection, Jet Set Chevron print
page 135: Spring 2019 "The Tourist" collection, Narcissus Border print

pages 136–137: Spring 2019 "The Tourist" collection, Big Narcissus print

page 138: Summer 2018 "California Dreaming" collection, Breeze Block Floral print
page 139: Spring 2017 "Havana" collection, Coppelia print

page 140: Spring 2019 "The Tourist" collection, Souvenir Stripe print
page 141: Spring 2018 "Superbloom" collection, Secret Garden print

page 142: Spring 2013 "Surf & Racquet Club" collection, Garden Maze print
page 143: Spring 2019 "The Tourist" collection, Fly-over Floral print

page 147: Cooper Design Space Los Angeles showroom seating area with plywood furniture designed by Bestor Architecture, silk tussah pillows, and vintage textile art by Romeo Reyna. Photo by Laure Joliet

page 148: Spring 2007 Pisces print on display in the Los Angeles showroom. Tom Dixon pendant light, Saarinen table, and Gio Ponti chairs by Cassina
page 149: Paned glass wall mimics the exterior windows. Plywood and laminate built-ins with hot pink industrial carpeting and vintage Steelcase office chairs. Design by Bestor Architecture, photo by Laure Joliet

page 151: Acid-yellow vestibule at the back of the original Palm Springs boutique with vintage chandelier, glass topped table, wicker flower chair and foiled wallpaper ceiling, 2002. Store design by Kelly Wearstler, photo by Grey Crawford

pages 152–153: Palm Springs store expansion included a Residential department displaying decorative items and textiles for the home, 2012. Store design by Bestor Architecture, photo by Lisa Romerein

page 154: When your dress matches your loveseat. The Peacock Ikat print in the first iteration of Trina Turk Residential, Palm Springs, CA, 2009. Store design by Phillip K. Smith III, photo by John Ellis
page 155: Palm Springs store expansion included a Mr Turk department, 2012. Store design by Bestor Architecture, photo by Lisa Romerein

page 156: Palm Springs flagship boutique window with San Jacinto Mountains in the background, 2009. Photo by John Ellis
page 157: Swimwear in the Palm Springs flagship. Store design by Bestor Architecture, photo by Lisa Romerein

pages 158–159: 25th Anniversary windows featuring a rainbow of looks from the archive and Trina's closet in Palm Springs, CA, 2020. Photo by Dan Chavkin

page 161: Eighty glass globe light fixtures in the central area of the original Los Angeles boutique, 2003. Store design by Kelly Wearstler, photo by Art Gray

page 162: Pink moiré wallpaper and Hollywood Regency details at the original Los Angeles boutique, 2003. Store design by Kelly Wearstler, photo by Art Gray
page 163: Vintage jewelry case, Crazy Botanical print dress and orange handbag, Spring 2004. Store design by Kelly Wearstler, photo by John Coolidge

page 164: Resort 2003 striped ponchos in the Los Angeles boutique. Photo by Art Gray
page 165: Spring 2004 in the angled glass windows of the original Los Angeles boutique. Photo by Art Gray

page 167: Dressing room in the New York boutique. Jonathan Adler chair and birdhouse, and a table from the estate of Bonnie Cashin with Spring 2007 Supercharm print dress. Store design by Jonathan Adler, photo by Eric Laignel

pages 168–169: Spring 2007 in the New York boutique. Store design by Jonathan Adler, photo by Eric Laignel

page 171: Cash wrap in the Bal Harbour shops boutique, with silk tussah wallcovering, vintage Jeré sunbursts and Spring 2010 accessories. Store design by MR Architecture + Decor, photo by Eric Laignel

page 172: Vintage mannequin head with Spring 2010 accessories and vintage Jeré sunburst in the Bal Harbour shops boutique
page 173: Seating area at Bal Harbour shops boutique. Store design by MR Architecture + Decor, photo by Eric Laignel

page 175: Summer 2017 in the Larchmont boutique. Store design by Bestor Architecture, photo by John Ellis

pages 176–177: Summer 2017 Mr Turk in the Larchmont boutique. Store design by Bestor Architecture, photo by John Ellis

page 179: Trina in vintage Pauline Trigère on the upper deck of the Ship of the Desert in Palm Springs, CA. Photo by Jonathan Skow

pages 180–181: The Streamline Moderne Ship of the Desert in Palm Springs, CA. Photo by Tim Street-Porter

page 182: Trina and Jonathan in the curved stairwell of the Ship of the Desert in Palm Springs, CA, 2010. Photo by Coral von Zumwalt
page 183: Dinner by the pool in Palm Springs, 2010. Photo by Coral von Zumwalt

page 184: Living room with vintage Vladimir Kagan sectional, Van Keppel-Green coffee table, Christofle silver wine cooler. Photo by Nicole LaMotte
page 185: Master bedroom with built-in loveseat and curved exterior deck. Vintage fiber art lion head by Judee du Bourdieu. Photo by Tim Street-Porter

page 186: Built-in booth in the kitchen with vintage Warren McArthur stools. Photo by Nicole LaMotte
page 187: Summer 2014 ikat caftan with Trina Turk embroidered pillows and vintage furnishings. Photo by Nicole LaMotte

page 189: Los Feliz backyard, 2007. 1950s Jean Touret by Atelier Marolles table, bench and chairs. Wayne Husted for Blenko Vineyard tumblers. Photo by Roger Davies

pages 190–191: Backyard view. Vintage Hall Bradley for Brown Jordan Alumicane patio furniture with Trina Turk Indoor/Outdoor for Schumacher Arches print cushions. Photo by Roger Davies

page 192: Front entryway with Jae Carmichael "Freeway" painting on a vintage Widdicomb mahogany credenza. Photo by Roger Davies
page 193: Living room built-ins with Jacques Adnet bar cart, yellow woven leather chair by Antonio Citterio, Klean mixed media collage, Wingate Paine photograph. Photo by Roger Davies

pages 194–195: Living room with Edward Wormley for Dunbar couch, Richard Neutra coffee table, 1920s Persian Mashad rug, brass chairs by Weiman/Warren Lloyd for Mastercraft, and rattan ottoman by Franco Albini for Vittorio Bonacina. Photo by Roger Davies

page 196: Guest room with Widdicomb dresser, Karl Springer side table, and lacquered vintage bed. Photo by Roger Davies
page 197: Vintage George Nelson dining table, vintage obis as a table runner, bronze X-back Billy Haines dining chairs. Photo by Bonnie Tsang

page 199: Facing west in Summer 2017 Gingko print. Photo by Jake Michaels

pages 200–201: Dining room with Jean Touret by Atelier Marolles dining set, Claire Falkenstein sculpture, and Tuareg mat. Photo by Jake Michaels

pages 202–203: Carport at the John Lautner-designed Salkin House in Echo Park, Los Angeles, CA. Photo by Laure Joliet

pages 204–205: Living room with vintage Albini rattan ottoman, slatted teak globe lounge chair, Chiwara headdresses, Richard Neutra coffee table, and Gerard Van Den Berg for Montis leather sofa. Photo by Gaelle Le Boulicaut

page 206: Vintage Robsjohn-Gibbings chair by Widdicomb and moroccan rug. Photo by Laure Joliet
page 207: Kitchen with redwood cabinetry and original 1940s oven. Photo by Laure Joliet

page 209: Built-in couch and shelves. Woodwork designed and crafted by Joseph Esherick with vintage Brent Bennett lamp. Photo by Paul Kozal

page 210: Living room from above with vintage chairs and tile-topped table. John Leslie mirrors. Photo by Paul Kozal
page 211: Looking west toward the ocean. Photo by Paul Kozal

pages 212–213: Spring 2011 "Palm Springs Eternal" collection, Cactus Flower print

page 215: Palm Springs Art Museum Architecture and Design Center opening party, 2014. Photo by John Ellis

page 216: 25th Anniversary Sunrise Ombré floral print Arco Iris dress and vintage hat in Oxnard, CA, 2019. Photo by Dewey Nicks

page 224: Sunnylands, Rancho Mirage, CA, 2013. Photo by Jonathan Skow

# TRINA TURK

Essays by Trina Turk, Simon Doonan, Booth Moore, Barbara Bestor

Edited and art directed by Gloria Fowler
Copyedited by Sara Richmond
Prepress by John Bailey at iocolor, LLC, Seattle, WA
Production by Kayleigh Jankowski

All photographs © their respective owners
All prints appearing in this book are copyrights of L2T, Inc. dba Trina Turk
© 2019 Chronicle Books LLC. All rights reserved.
No part of this book may be reproduced in any form without
prior written permission from the publisher.

ISBN: 978-1-7972-0384-3
Library of Congress Cataloging-in-Publication Data available.

Manufactured in China

 CHRONICLE CHROMA

Chronicle Chroma is an imprint of Chronicle Books
Los Angeles, California

chroniclechroma.com